Ready, Set, Remote!

The Fast Guide to Creating a
Professional Home Office

Dave Allen

Contents

1st Edition 2023

2nd edition 2024

Preface: What This Book Is About

C reating an efficient home office requires careful consideration of various factors that can impact your work experience. From ergonomic challenges to potential distractions, ensuring a productive and comfortable remote work environment is crucial.

Ergonomics plays a pivotal role in your well-being. Ignoring the importance of proper chair support, desk height, and adequate lighting can lead to physical discomfort and health issues. Additionally, the home environment comes with distractions – family members, pets, or household chores can disrupt your focus and hinder productivity. Blurring boundaries between work and personal life is a common struggle, potentially leading to overworking and increased stress. Isolation is another concern, as working from home could lead to a lack of socialization, impacting your mental well-being and motivation.

Then, there are the technical challenges like unreliable internet connections and outdated equipment, which can obstruct your workflow.

Ensuring the security of sensitive information in a home setting is also critical, requiring careful consideration of cybersecurity measures.

Imagine a home office where ergonomic considerations are prioritized, ensuring your physical well-being and comfort. Envision a workspace free from distractions, allowing you to concentrate fully on your tasks. Picture a seamless and secure technology setup, promoting efficient communication and collaboration with your team. Visualize a well-defined work-life balance with clear boundaries and dedicated spaces for both professional and personal activities.

To achieve this ideal home office, I'll show you proactive steps. You'll learn about ergonomic furniture and setting up a dedicated workspace to enhance your physical comfort and focus. Along the way, you'll establish clear boundaries for work hours and personal time, creating a distinct separation between the two. You'll understand how to upgrade your technology and how to implement and prioritize cybersecurity. We'll introduce virtual networking opportunities to overcome the limitations of remote work. And we'll emphasize mental health by incorporating breaks and self-care into your routine.

Taking decisive actions can transform your home office into a conducive and thriving workspace that supports your professional and personal well-being.

Introduction: Navigating the Home Office Odyssey

O ne of my favorite TV programs is the Discovery Channel's "Expedition Unknown" with Josh Gates. I've always enjoyed how Josh takes exploring seriously but always adds his spark of humor to make each episode more fun and endearing. I wanted to inject some of that jocularity into my presentation as well. I'm no Josh Gates, but welcome to the grand expedition of remote work, the saga of home office mastery, the quest for productivity, and balance in the virtual realm. And as for the touch of humor, the puns and Dad jokes begin now- you've been warned! Along our journey, you'll become an explorer, time traveler, superhero, circus ringleader, and ultimately a remote work warrior. At the same time, we'll transform your home office from a mere space into a powerhouse of productivity and joy.

Acknowledgments: ChatGPT was my writing assistant in creating this journey. It was my first use of this brilliant technology, and it was an immense help in overcoming writer's block, assisting in research, and helping smooth out some rough spots—also, Canva, Grammarly, and Pexels. Kindlepreneur was a brilliant source for educational and publishing resources in bringing this book to life. I also want to thank Publishing.com; without their assistance and motivation, I may not have ventured into writing.

About Me: As you'll soon discover, no virtual meeting is conducted without a quick introduction of yourself. So, my first piece of advice is to develop an "Elevator Speech" for introductions. It will avoid awkward silences as you try to tell everyone what you do while avoiding a lengthy description. Here's mine:

"Hi everyone; I'm Dave Allen, a Customer Success Manager on the team for a couple of years now. I'm a helicopter pilot and have flown air ambulances and for TV news, but I also have jet experience with the airlines and am a retired US Army Major. My hobbies are Aviation, playing horse polo, and wearing pants to virtual meetings."

Okay, I made up the last bit about pants, but I told you the Dad-Jokes would be prevalent in this book, and so it begins. Looking at the introduction, you'll notice it was fast and to the point. It covered the high points of my qualifications and a little about me personally. There's no need for a life history here, and a great conversation starter for the future as people desire to get to know you better.

"Wait. Dave is a pilot?" you may ask yourself, "What makes a pilot qualified to tell me about creating a home office?"

As of this writing, my current employer is a worldwide company of a product for pilots to help them plan and navigate the skies. So, as a Customer Success Manager for them, I'm a work-from-home pilot! Customer Success is a relative newcomer to the business scene and manages the customer journey through the post-sale environment. The team works with clients to increase retention and help them on their journey through onboarding and introducing new or additional products, helping them increase productivity.

I also mentioned that I was a TV News pilot. I flew and reported (yes, while flying the helicopter) for TV News in northern California. I studied Radio and Television Production in college, and over the years, I've produced training videos and worked in TV studios. This experience helped when it came time to create my home office, which I affectionately refer to as my "Set". Along with that experience, I owned an aerial photography company years before drones were common.

To round things out, I've also owned transportation companies in the form of limousines and taxicabs. So, as you can see, I'm no stranger to working from home, consulting with clients, and generally having fun meeting people in many different business settings.

And now, I'm ready to help you as you begin your journey into remote work. Whether full-time, part-time, or as a side gig, you'll gain the insight to set up a fabulous home office to enhance your remote work productivity.

Onward, intrepid explorers, to the grand expedition of mastering the home office and thriving in the virtual realm!

"This is your captain speaking. Fasten your seatbelts. We're ready for takeoff!"

Dave

Chapter One

Understanding the Landscape

W elcome to the wild world of remote work, where your commute involves navigating through a traffic jam of kid toys, and the coffee shop always has your favorite brands. If you're reading this, you've likely swapped your office cubicle for your home's cozy (sometimes chaotic) confines, or you soon will. Congratulations! You've just embarked on a journey that requires a bit of strategic thinking, a dash of humor, and the uncanny ability to ignore the siren call of your comfy couch during working hours.

The world of remote work isn't just about avoiding dress codes and stealing cuddles from your furry coworkers (yes, pets count as coworkers now). It's a realm of unprecedented freedom and flexibility, replete with its own set of challenges. In this chapter, we will unpack the remote work landscape, climb its virtual peaks, and stumble into a few online meeting valleys along the way.

The Evolution of Remote Work: From Office Chains to Home Freedom

Growing up at the tail end of the Boomer generation, "working from home" was a euphemism for catching up on favorite sitcoms in pajamas. It's more or less like a sick day from school. Well, times have changed, my friend. Remote work has evolved from a quirky notion to a full-blown lifestyle. We're not just breaking free from office chains; we're redefining what work means.

In the not-so-good old days, you had to clock in and out at the office and remain there for most of the workday. You now get to leave that behind. Your time is now yours; your office is wherever your Wi-Fi signal reaches. It's liberating, empowering, and occasionally bewildering. But fear not, intrepid remote worker, because I'm about to fly you to this brave new world. Of course, I'll have to inject the aviation aphorisms in here. Pilot. Remember?

The Benefits and Challenges of Home Offices: Where Comfort Meets Chaos

Let's talk perks. No more soul-crushing commutes. Your office attire can range from business casual to "I-woke-up-like-this chic." The savings on razor blades alone make everything worth it. And coffee breaks? They happen in your kitchen, with *your* brand of coffee, and no judgment if you take the last pastry. If anyone does object, you can always respond with "Hey! I'm working here!"

But, ah, the challenges. Distractions lurk around every corner, from the comfy couch and weighted blanket to the ever-growing pile of dishes in the sink. And let's not mention the daily battle with technology that somehow transforms into an epic saga when you least expect it.

This book will dive into the good, the bad, and the "Whoever is eating lunch, could you mute?" of home offices. We'll strategize and hopefully laugh together, but the only tear you'll shed will be chopping onions for dinner if you're reading this on your Kindle or from my humor. It's known to have that effect on occasion.

We're about to embark on an expedition to redefine how you work, one cozy corner of your home at a time. Get ready for a jungle raft ride through the twists and turns of freedom and rocky rapids of a never-ending to-do list. Welcome to the wild world of remote work – it's a jungle here, but together, we'll swing from the vines and conquer the virtual landscape. Tarzan yells, and chest-thumping optional.

The first step will be to identify your home office space. Please, my friends, get the heck out of the kitchen! You're a professional, and your background should reflect your job, so unless you're a chef, the kitchen is hereby off-limits!

Your space should be a place you can close yourself off, preferably with a lockable door. Ask yourself, how often do you use that guestroom? Once in a blue moon? As a home office, it gets used daily and becomes a tax deduction!

Chapter Two

Ergonomics: A Foundation for Success

A lright, fellow home office adventurers, grab your Fedora's (AKA the Indiana Jones hat) because we're swinging on that vine into the world of ergonomics. I know what you're thinking: "Ergo-what now?" Don't worry; it's not as complicated as it sounds. Ergonomics is the magic that turns your workspace from a pain in the back (literally) to a productivity powerhouse.

Importance of Ergonomics in the Home Office: Upfront Information about your back

Let's get real for a moment. Your back has been through a lot – long hours at the kitchen table, hunched over like a gargoyle, and the occasional "I'll just answer these emails from the couch" situation. It's time to get things straight between you and your spine. Ergonomics is about setting up your workspace so your body doesn't scream at you by lunchtime.

Picture this: a chair that cradles your back like a supportive friend, a desk that doesn't make you feel like a five-year-old at the dinner table when reaching for your keyboard, and a screen large enough so you're not forced into a perpetual game of "guess where the cursor is."

Selecting the Right Furniture and Equipment: Because Your Body Deserves the VIP Treatment

Now, I'm not saying you need to drop a month's rent on a fancy ergonomic chair that looks like it's from a sci-fi movie (although, if you can, go for it). We're talking practical upgrades here – a chair that doesn't double as a medieval torture device, a desk that doesn't wobble like a Jenga tower, and a keyboard that won't leave your wrists feeling like they just ran a marathon. Ergonomics is about not using that laptop keyboard, which will have your neck bent downward for ages. Set that whole laptop on a stand with an external keyboard and keep the screen at eye level. Trust me, your neck and back will grant a standing ovation just for that.

It's all about creating a setup that suits you. Think of it as customizing your character in a video game. Your equipment should cater to your unique stats and playstyle.

Be choosy when choosing a chair! Let that be your mantra as you conduct your search. Be very careful about selecting a seat online. You will use this daily and for hours on end (embrace the pun!). Indeed, you can research online, but I suggest heading to the store and sitting in different models. Then, if you can find the same one cheaper online, and your store won't price match, you can order the delivery.

In no particular order, here are four highly regarded home office chairs known for their ergonomic design, comfort, and durability:

1. Herman Miller Aeron:

- Features: The Herman Miller Aeron is a widely recognized ergonomic chair known for its comfortable mesh design and adjustable features. It offers excellent lumbar support and a variety of adjustment options, and it is suitable for long hours of sitting.

- Adjustability: Fully adjustable arms, seat height, and tilt

- Material: Mesh (I like mesh. It allows airflow around you and keeps you from getting too hot when sitting for extended periods.)

2. Steelcase Leap Chair:

- Features: The Steelcase Leap Chair is praised for its exceptional ergonomic design, providing good support for the lower back and accommodating various sitting postures. It has a flexible backrest and a LiveBack technology that adjusts to your movements.

- Adjustability: Adjustable arms, seat depth, and lower back firmness

- Material: Fabric or leather options

3. Secretlab Omega Series:

- Features: The Secretlab Omega Series is a gaming chair that has gained popularity for its ergonomic design and comfort. It features lumbar support, a reclining function, and memory foam cushions. While designed for gaming, it's also suitable for long office hours.

- Adjustability: Adjustable armrests, recline, and lumbar support

- Material: PU leather or fabric options

4. IKEA Markus:

- Features: The IKEA Markus is a more budget-friendly option providing comfort and support. It has a high backrest, adjustable headrest, and lumbar support. While it may have fewer features than some high-end chairs, it offers solid value for the price.

- Adjustability: Adjustable seat height and tilt tension

- Material: Fabric or leather options

Consider factors such as lumbar support, adjustable features, material, and style when choosing a home office chair, and find a chair that suits your body type and provides the necessary support for extended periods of sitting.

Are you a keyboard warrior? Choosing the best home office keyboard depends on your preferences and needs. Here are some popular options that cater to different preferences (also in no particular order):

1. Logitech MX Keys:

- Features: The MX Keys is known for its comfortable typing experience, backlit keys, and compatibility with multiple devices. It also has a sleek design and durable build quality.

2. Ducky One 2 Mini:

- Features: The Ducky One 2 Mini is a popular choice if you prefer a compact mechanical keyboard. It's known for its customizable RGB lighting and high-quality Cherry MX switches.

3. Corsair K95 RGB Platinum XT:

- Features: This high-end mechanical keyboard has customizable RGB lighting, dedicated media controls, and programmable macro keys. It's suitable for both gaming and office use.

4. Microsoft Ergonomic Keyboard:

- Features: The Microsoft Ergonomic Keyboard is a good choice if you prioritize comfort and ergonomic design. It has a split design and a cushioned palm rest for a more natural typing position.

5. Apple Magic Keyboard:

- Features: If you're in the Apple ecosystem, the Magic Keyboard is a sleek, wireless option that pairs well with Macs and iPads. It offers a comfortable typing experience and a low-profile design.

When choosing a keyboard, consider factors such as the type of work you do, your typing preferences, whether you prefer mechanical or membrane switches (clicky or soft press), and any additional features you may need. You should also consider how much noise the keyboard makes when typing. You don't want to wake up the family with the loud clatter of furiously typing an email or report late at night. Just like with chairs, try out keyboards in-store to get a feel for the typing experience before making a decision.

And since you'll have an external keyboard, let's consider an external monitor. It reduces eye strain and allows more workspace for moving around all those communication channels, browsers, and open emails. It makes online meetings much nicer when you can see the presentation. Additionally, if you plan to use the monitor for video conferencing, built-in webcams and integrated speakers might be vital features to consider.

Selecting the best monitor for your home office depends on your needs, such as screen size, resolution, connectivity options, and budget. Once again, in no particular order, here are three highly regarded monitors that offer a combination of quality features:

1. Dell UltraSharp U2720Q:

- Features: The Dell UltraSharp U2720Q is a 27-inch 4K monitor known for its excellent color accuracy and crisp image quality. Its USB-C port provides easy connectivity with laptops, and its thin bezels offer a modern look. The monitor suits tasks requiring detailed visuals, such as content creation and design work.

- Resolution: 4K UHD (3840 x 2160)

- Connectivity: HDMI, DisplayPort, USB-C

2. LG 27UD88-W:

- Features: The LG 27UD88-W is a 27-inch 4K monitor that combines a sleek design with features like FreeSync for gaming. It offers vibrant colors and supports USB-C connectivity for video and data transfer. The on-screen control feature allows for easy customization of monitor settings.

- Resolution: 4K UHD (3840 x 2160)

- Connectivity: HDMI, DisplayPort, USB-C

3. BenQ PD3220U:

- Features: The BenQ PD3220U is a 32-inch 4K monitor focusing on professional design and content creation. It has factory calibration for accurate color reproduction, HDR support, and a KVM switch for easy switching between multiple devices. The larger screen size can enhance productivity for users who need more screen real estate.

- Resolution: 4K UHD (3840 x 2160)

- Connectivity: HDMI, DisplayPort, Thunderbolt 3 (USB-C)

When choosing a monitor, consider your typical usage, the color accuracy required, and the available desk space. Always check the specifications and reviews to ensure the monitor meets your requirements.

A note for Macbook users: Mac has specific monitors on their Ecosystem. If you have a Mac, check for compatibility when searching for a monitor. All the monitors mentioned in the previous list are compatible with MacBooks. They have various connectivity options, including USB-C or Thunderbolt 3, commonly found on modern MacBooks.

Do you love to stretch out while you work? Stop eyeballing that couch! I'm talking about a standing desk to conquer deadlines while conquering your smartwatch goals. There are even treadmill desks for adventurous people who are not me.

Selecting the best standing desk for your home office involves considering factors such as adjustability, stability, build quality, and aesthetics. Here are four standing desks that are well-regarded for their features. Can you guess what order they're in?

1. Fully Jarvis Bamboo Standing Desk:

- Features: The Fully Jarvis Bamboo Standing Desk is famous for its solid build quality, smooth height adjustments, and environmentally friendly bamboo surface. It offers a wide range of customization options and comes with a digital display handset for easy adjustments.

- Adjustability: Electric height adjustment with memory presets

- Material: Bamboo or laminate options

2. Uplift V2 Standing Desk:

- Features: The Uplift V2 Standing Desk is known for its stability and durability. It has a strong frame, various desktop materials and sizes, and advanced features such as a height memory keypad. The desk also offers optional accessories like power outlets and wire management solutions.

- Adjustability: Electric height adjustment with memory presets

- Material: Various desktop options including bamboo, laminate, and rubberwood

3. Varidesk ProDesk 60 Electric:

- Features: The Varidesk ProDesk 60 Electric is an electric standing desk with a spacious desktop. It's known for its sturdy construction, quiet electric motors, and ease of assembly. The desk offers a simple yet effective solution for those transitioning between sitting and standing during work hours.

- Adjustability: Electric height adjustment with memory presets

- Material: Laminate

4. Steelcase Ology Height-Adjustable Desk:

- Features: The Steelcase Ology Height-Adjustable Desk is a premium option known for its advanced features and ergonomic design. It has a responsive lift mechanism, cable management solutions, and anti-collision technology for safety. The desk design supports health and well-being in the workplace.

- Adjustability: Electric height adjustment with anti-collision technology

- Material: Laminate or veneer options

Additionally, when choosing a standing desk, consider the available space, the weight it can support, and whether it meets your ergonomic needs. Some desks have optional accessories like cable management, keyboard trays, and monitor arms to enhance your overall workspace setup.

Creating a Comfortable and Productive Workspace: Where Magic Happens (Without needing a wand)

Now that you've got the right gear, let's discuss the magic ingredient: organization. Although we're on an expedition to create the home office, you don't want your desk to be a jungle. A cluttered desk is like a jungle – you might look for treasure but get lost and attacked by a wild stapler. Keep it tidy, friends, and consider this your official permission to splurge on desk organizers, cable management solutions, and maybe a motivational desk plant (they're excellent listeners). When your workspace is a haven of order and good vibes, you'll be amazed at how it boosts your focus and creativity. You'll finally have a home for that collection of quirky pens you've hoarded.

So, my newly transformed ergonomic enthusiasts, let's create a sanctuary of comfort and productivity. Your back, neck, and overall sanity will thank you. Prepare to conquer the ergonomic quest – it's time to level up your home office game!

Chapter Three

Conquering Distractions

What jungle expedition would be complete without seeing an elephant? And here's one now! Let's talk about the room-filling elephant we all face in our daily quests – distractions. Distractions are the arch-nemesis of productivity, whether it's the alluring call of the pantry, the irresistible lure of social media, or the sudden urge to reorganize your sock drawer. Learning to conquer distractions can be a lot to digest, but fear not, brave soul, for we shall, as the saying goes, eat this elephant one bite at a time.

Identifying Common Distractions in a Home Environment: Oooooh, Shiney!

Distractions come in all shapes and sizes and often wear cunning disguises –the pile of dishes winking at you from the sink, the couch that beckons with open arms (yes, the comfy couch is mentioned a lot. It's my nemesis), and the home team loudly arguing over what to watch. Not to mention the internet itself. One minute, you're diligently researching for your latest presenttation, and the next, you're knee-deep in a YouTube rabbit hole of cat videos. Been there. Done that. Shrank the T-Shirt. I knew I shouldn't have subscribed to that laundry tips channel.

Strategies for Maintaining Focus and Productivity

Now that we've identified the distractions, it's time to slice through the jungle. Picture this: a whip of discipline (don't go there; it's a safari metaphor), a machete of focus, and a Fedora of noise-canceling headphones (because, let's face it, your neighbor's love for lawn mowing is not helping your productivity).

Schedule your time just as you would in a company office. A calendar program works great, and your company probably uses Microsoft Teams or Google Calendar to schedule your time. If you're self-employed, either of those still works great. Even a pen-and-paper appointment book works well for scheduling. But don't just make it; use it. Self-discipline is the key to working from home. Stick to the schedule you create, and when joining online meetings, remember if you're on time, you're late. Always log in about three minutes before the scheduled time. Your calendar will help you navigate the sea of time management that will unexpectedly become high-tide you if you don't use a schedule.

Designate specific breaks to tend to personal matters so you're not sneaking off to fold laundry during a conference call. You can even put home chores into the calendar if you like. Just be realistic about how long they take. And yes, the opposite is also true: resist the urge to check work emails when you should be enjoying your well-deserved downtime.

So, crack that whip, machete through the vines of distractions and emerge from this jungle as masters of concentration. The distractions may try to lure us into their lairs, but we shall prevail and emerge with productivity banners held high. And remember, when eating the elephant, there are no leftovers!

Chapter Four

The Social Side of Remote Work

A nd the next adventure shall be into the territory of the social side of remote work. Working from home doesn't mean you have to turn into a hermit. It's time to trade the solitude for some virtual high-fives and digital camaraderie.

Combating Isolation: Building Virtual Connections

Isolation, meet your match: the power of virtual connections. While it's tempting to wrap yourself in a blanket fort and communicate exclusively in emojis, that's not the best recipe for mental well-being. Reaching out to your colleagues through the magical wonders of video calls and messaging apps is okay. It's like having a water cooler chat without the questionable office coffee.

Pro tip: Schedule virtual coffee breaks. It's the perfect excuse to flaunt your quirky mug collection and discuss the latest streaming obsessions. Your isolation-fighting sidekick? A good old-fashioned happy hour. Meet with a cherished co-worker virtually for an hour after work. You can even let it go a little longer because sometimes, a happy hour deserves more than just one hour. Or more than one glass of wine.

Strategies for Remote Team Collaboration: Turning Virtual Teamwork into a Superpower

Teamwork makes the dream work, and that dream is even more fantastical when everyone spans different time zones. Our expeditionary force carries a backpack of collaboration tools as our trusty companions. Dive into the world of shared documents, collaborative project management platforms, and video conferencing. Your company probably dictates what you use, but if not, there are many tools to choose from. Google Meet, Webex, Slack, and Zoom. Dropbox, Microsoft 365/ OneDrive, Amazon Drive, Trello, and others are all designed to help you collaborate with your team. Too many to choose? Pick one from each category, like Zoom, Slack, and Dropbox, and then train yourself to become an expert in each one. Once you have something you know, you can branch out to others.

Fostering a Positive Remote Work Culture: Because We're All in This Together

Culture is like the secret sauce that makes remote work bearable and downright enjoyable. Cultivate a positive atmosphere by celebrating achievements, big or small. Build small wins into each project and celebrate each minor victory on the way to completion.

Encourage open communication (Slack is excellent for this). Your team is navigating the same uncharted waters; sometimes, a well-placed GIF can express more than a hundred words. And remember, laughter is the best medicine – share memes, jokes, and funny anecdotes. A well-timed dad joke can be the hero your virtual meeting needs. I speak from experience.

So, brave pioneers of the remote realm, let's make this digital landscape our playground. Combat isolation with virtual hangouts, turn remote collaboration into a superpower and foster a positive culture that transcends the pixels on your screen.

Chapter Five

Overcoming Technical Hurdles

G et your swim trunks (no speedos, please) because we're diving headfirst into the realm of ones and zeros, pixels, and cables – yes, it's time to conquer the mighty technical hurdles that come with working from home. We shall not let the spinning wheel of doom or the Blue Screen of Death defeat us!

Addressing Internet and Equipment Challenges: Navigating the Digital Wilderness

Have you ever felt like your Wi-Fi has a vendetta against productivity? Join the club. We've all been stuck in the buffering zone when you just need to upload that crucial document.

First, a reliable internet connection is your trusty steed in this digital quest. Invest in the best one your budget can handle. Home internet comes in two parts: the gateway and the router. The Gateway is just what it says: it brings the internet into your home. The Router is what distributes the internet throughout your home. The internet company usually provides the Gateway, and some, like Cellular Home Internet, offer free Gateways (some are even Gateway/Router combos). When shopping for internet service, there is a phrase to remember: "speeds _up to_". Just because a company says it has the fastest speed _up to_ a gigabyte doesn't mean that's the speed you'll experience at home.

Don't fall for this. I paid for Gig speed for a long time but noticed things didn't seem that fast. I ordered some home internet from a cellular provider and, for two months, made speed comparisons (it's easy to do with an online search for "test my internet speed"). Lo and behold, the cellular internet was precisely the same speed as my so-called Gig-Intenet, at one-third the price! I canceled the expensive one and have been sailing smoothly for two years.

Your router sends the internet signal to your entire house. They also provide another layer of security. Consider an upgrade if your router resembles an ancient tech museum relic. The internet should be your ally, not the mischievous trickster it often pretends to be.

The latest protocol is WIFI 6. Don't confuse it with 5G. They're separate things, and too much to go into here. Just know that selecting the best home office router depends on factors such as the size of your home, the number of devices connected, the internet speed you subscribe to, and specific features you may need. As of my last knowledge update in January 2022, here are some highly regarded home office routers:

1. ASUS RT-AX88U:

- Features: The ASUS RT-AX88U is a high-performance Wi-Fi 6 router with advanced features. It offers fast speeds, multiple antennas

for extended coverage, and features like MU-MIMO and beamform-
ing. The router is suitable for homes with many devices and demand-
ing networking needs.

2. NETGEAR Nighthawk AX12 (RAX120):

- Features: The NETGEAR Nighthawk AX12 is a Wi-Fi 6 router
known for its high-speed capabilities and wide coverage. It comes
with multiple antennas, support for multiple devices, and features like
Dynamic QoS for optimized gaming and streaming.

3. TP-Link Archer AX6000:

- Features: The TP-Link Archer AX6000 is a dual-band Wi-Fi 6 router
with impressive speeds and various features. It includes multiple Gi-
gabit Ethernet ports, USB ports for network-attached storage (NAS),
and HomeCare security features for added protection.

4. Google Nest WiFi:

- Features: The Google Nest WiFi is known for its ease of use and mesh
networking capabilities. It comprises a router and additional points
placed around your home for extended coverage. It's a good choice for
those looking for a simple, reliable solution with the added benefit of
a smart speaker in each unit.

5. Eero Pro 6:

- Features: The Eero Pro 6 is a Wi-Fi 6 mesh system focusing on
simplicity and reliable coverage. It supports multiple devices and additional units for seamless mesh networking. It's a good option for
users who prioritize easy setup and reliability.

I've used both Google Nest and Eero Pro 6. Both were easy to use, but I prefer the Eero. It's just the most hassle-free router I've ever used. Note that the Nighthawk mentioned gaming. Generally, you can view companies that optimize for gaming to be of the highest quality but often the highest price. Gamers take their hobby seriously, and Netgear has been at the top of their equipment list for many years.

Before deciding, it's essential to assess your specific requirements and check for any updates or newer models that may have been released since my last update. Additionally, consider whether you need features such as VPN support, parental controls, or advanced security options when choosing a router for your home office.

Cybersecurity Best Practices for the Home Office: Guarding Your Digital Castle

Your home is your castle, and your digital kingdom deserves the same protection. Cybersecurity might sound like a medieval incantation, but you must keep your data safe from the virtual road agents out there.

Equip your castle with strong passwords, the kind even a supercomputer would struggle to crack. Update your software and antivirus programs religiously – consider it a digital shield upgrade. And beware of phishing scams; not every email is a friendly messenger. The best defense is to look at who is sending the email, and if it doesn't seem right, it probably isn't. Never click on a link in an email unless you request it, even if it looks like it comes from a friend or a company you do business with. Criminals are beginning to use Artificial Intelligence now, and they are getting very good at appearing legitimate. This is why I'm not including links in this book. I don't want to run the risk they could be hijacked or otherwise broken. To stay up on the latest internet scams, go to the FBI Website. Do an online search for FBI Common Scams, and you'll find the site.

Optimizing Your Tech Setup for Seamless Work: Turning Your Devices into Sidekicks

Okay, enough of the serious stuff. Let's talk about devices. Your laptop isn't just a tool; it's your trusty sidekick in this digital adventure. Keep it running smoothly with regular maintenance – declutter that desktop, organize your files, and maybe give it a metaphorical pat on the back (or a literal one, if you're feeling whimsical). You can even give them names now. Search for "How to Name My PC (or Mac)".

Explore the wonders of productivity apps and tools. From project management platforms to time-tracking apps, there's a digital wizardry solution for every workflow woe. Embrace the tech arsenal at your disposal, and you'll wield the machete of efficiency in no time.

So, fellow tech adventurers, let's face these digital dragons head-on. Strengthen your internet fortress, fortify your cybersecurity defenses, and turn your devices into loyal sidekicks. The technical hurdles might try to throw a glitch in our plans, but armed with knowledge, we shall emerge victorious in the digital realm. Onward to tech glory!

Chapter Six

Balancing Act: Work-Life Harmony

T he art of balancing work and personal life may appear to require a superhero to conquer. But faster than a speeding bullet, you will soon leap the tall building that is the secret to achieving that elusive work-life harmony. Your new superhero persona is The Resilience Avenger!

Establishing Clear Boundaries: Because Even Superheroes Need Rest

Creating a superhero-worthy work-life harmony starts with setting boundaries. Your caped crusader persona is The Guardian of Time. As the Guardian of Time, you will establish precise work hours and flourish the cape of closure when those hours are over. Shut down your work devices, step away from the virtual battlefield, and cry,

"Up, Up, and awaaaay!" as you exit your home office to enjoy some well-deserved downtime. I double-dog, dare ya.

Communicate these boundaries to your work teammates. Let them know that when the cape (or the Slack channel) is off, so are you. Of course, emergencies happen, but the all-night heroics that don't involve an all-hands-on-deck situation are reserved for actual super-heroes. Do this with the hometeam crew, too (yeah, the family). Tell them that when you're in your home office headquarters, especially in a meeting, you are not to be disturbed (unless it's an emergency or if someone has successfully brewed a fresh pot of coffee).

I purchased a door hangar that says, "Do not disturb. I'm on a call", and I hang it on the doorknob when I'm in meetings. I also know some tech-savvy people who replaced a light bulb in the hallway and have their smart device turn the bulb red when they don't want to be disturbed. If you clearly communicate when you'lll be on a break, and are reliable about taking them, you'll soon train the home team to respect your work time.

Overcoming Overwork and Burnout: A Quest for Self-Preservation

I read many different articles on burnout when researching this book. Depending on the varied sources, between 60% and 90% of US Work-ers suffer symptoms of burnout. NO matter how you look at it, the majority of us are experiencing burnout. It's may even be why you chose remote work. Burnout is the specter we all fear, lurking in the shadows, ready to pounce when our guard is down (or is that the fam-ily cat?). But with self-awareness and a hearty dose of self-compassion, we can vanquish this demon head-on.

Keep an eye out for the warning signs of burnout – exhaustion, irritability, and a sudden desire to switch careers and become a beach bum. When you hear the spirit whispering, take a step back. Delegate tasks, practice the ancient art of saying 'no,' and embrace the magical healing powers of breaks.

My boss has a great way of saying no. He calls it the "Positive No". The idea is to offer an alternative or concession along with your turn-down.

For instance, a customer asks, "Can I receive this service for free?"

A positive no would be to say: "I understand your request for a complimentary service. While I can't offer it for free, I can offer you a special promotion or package deal that includes additional benefits at a discounted rate. You can still enjoy our services while getting the best value. Would you like more details on these options?"

The emphasis is on acknowledging the customer's request, expressing understanding, and offering alternative solutions that align with their needs and preferences. This approach helps maintain a positive customer relationship even when you can't fulfill the initial request.

Great with clients, but what about with the boss or a coworker?

Boss: "Can you complete this project by the end of the week?"

Response:

"I appreciate the urgency of this project. Given the current workload, it might be challenging to meet the end-of-week deadline. However, I can provide a prioritized timeline and suggest which tasks to defer or delegate to ensure we meet the most critical aspects of the project by Friday. Does that work for you?"

Coworker: "Can you cover my shift next Saturday?"

Response:

"I understand you have a commitment on Saturday, and I wish I could help. Unfortunately, I have a prior engagement that day. However, I can check with other colleagues to see if someone can cover your shift or discuss potential alternatives with our manager. Let's find a solution together."

As with clients, emphasize acknowledging the request, expressing understanding, and offering alternative solutions that align with their needs and preferences.

Designing a Home Office with Work-Life Balance in Mind: Feng Shui for your hero headquarters

Your home office is not just a place to conquer deadlines; it's a sanctuary for achieving balance. Let's time-travel back to the nineteen-eighties to look for some ballance. When President Reagan visited to China in 1984, he brought back more than a couple of Pandas. His visit sparked an awareness in the USA of the ancient practice of Feng Shui. Feng Shui, the art of arranging your space for good vibes, is your secret superpower to combat burnout.

Position your desk for maximum energy flow, add a touch of greenery for balance, and consider the magical powers of natural light. A well-designed workspace is like a charm against the chaos of life, creating an environment where productivity and serenity can coexist. When I set up my office, I was tempted to put the desk in the traditional spot, the middle of the room, with the window at my back. Having been in the television industry, I knew any video camera hates light behind a subject. With a window behind you, all your clients and cohorts will see is a bright halo with a dark silhouette in the middle. I turned the desk around so it faced the window. I can now look outside whenever I need a minor distraction, and I have natural light on my face for the webcam— done and done.

So, let's return from the Regan years bringing along the two best things: Feng Shui and Eighties One-hit-Wonders. Set those boundaries like the superhero you are, be vigilant against the specter of burnout, and transform your home office into a haven of balance.

Embrace your inner Resilience Avenger, and may your journey lead you to triumph over the evil supervillan of burnout!

Chapter Seven

Family Matters: Juggling Work and Family Life

W ell, since our metaphorical references have spanned from explorers to superheroes, let's add another to the list. In this chapter, we'll head into the three-ring circus of family matters and the intricate art of juggling work and familial obligations. It's the big top, a magic show, and occasionally a sitcom all rolled into one. Let's don our imaginary capes, fedora's, or clown shoes (all three if you're adventurous) and venture into the chaotic yet heartwarming world of familial bliss and remote work.

Managing Childcare and Family Responsibilities: Where Every Day Is a New Juggling Act

First, for those of you who chose the aforementioned clown shoes, parenting while working from home has been described as juggling a dozen eggs while riding a unicycle on a tightrope. It's a delicate balancing act that requires focus, skill, and a lot of patience. One wrong move, and you'll end up with egg on your face (and keyboard). But don't worry, my friend! With the right mindset and a good sense of humor, you can master the art of parenting while working from home. Just remember to take it one egg at a time!

Create a schedule that aligns with your family's rhythm. Designate focused work periods and breaks for quality time with your pint-sized teammates. And if all else fails, consider bribery – I mean, positive reinforcement. Stickers and gold stars work wonders for both toddlers and adults.

Creating a Supportive Family Environment for Remote Work: Teamwork Makes the Dream Work

Your family is not just a bunch of cohabitants; they are your teammates in this grand adventure. Foster a supportive environment by communicating your work hours and enlisting your family's help respecting those boundaries. A "Do Not Disturb, Genius at Work" sign might be a worthy investment.

Involve your family in your work victories. Share your accomplishments, no matter how small, and let your kids in on the excitement. Who knew completing a spreadsheet could be as thrilling as a superhero showdown?

Strategies for Harmonizing Family and Professional Obligations: The Art of Synchronized Living

Harmonizing work and family life is akin to choreographing a dance routine – there's a rhythm, there are steps, and occasionally, someone steps on someone else's toes. But fear not, maestro of the family symphony; we've got some strategies up our sleeves.

Coordinate schedules with your partner if you have one. Tag-team parenting can transform the chaotic clown car of family life into a synchronized spectacle. Set realistic expectations and communicate openly about your workload and deadlines. Flexibility is vital, so embrace the beautiful chaos. Juggle those family responsibilities with finesse, creating a supportive family unit, and harmonize the melody of work and family life. It may be a circus, but it's your circus, and you're the ringmaster. Onward to the next act in this heartwarming family and work extravaganza!

Chapter Eight

Mental Wellness in the Home Office

S uperheros and circuses aside, let's return to our home office expedition, this time to blaze the trail through the elusive and essential realm of mental wellness in the home office. It's time to befriend your inner Zen master, so take a deep breath, exhale the stress, and trek through the art of maintaining sanity in the virtual universe.

Recognizing and Addressing Mental Health Challenges: Untangling the vines

Let's face it: the home office can be a breeding ground for mental health challenges. From the subtle whispers of imposter syndrome to the occasional visit from the anxiety monster, we've got some sneaky villains to unmask.

Recognize when these vines as they attempt to wind their way into your mental sancutary. Are you feeling overwhelmed, tired, or unmotivated? It's time to don the hat of mental health and address these challenges head-on. Remember, we all need help from time to time. The only failure is in not seeking it.

Incorporating Self-Care Practices: Because You Deserve It

Self-care isn't just a buzzword; it's your first line of defense against stress and burnout— self-care is the magical elixir that rejuvenates your mind and soul.

Create a self-care routine that suits your style – a morning meditation, an afternoon walk, a run, or an evening streaming binge (hey, we all have our methods). Create a ritual to signal the start and end of your workday. It could be how you brew your morning beverage or a victory dance to bid farewell to your tasks. Your mind associates rituals with focus, making your workspace a beacon of concentration and creativity and reducing the stress of home and work competing for your attention.

Seeking Support and Resources for Mental Well-being: Heroes Don't Go It Alone

Even superheroes need allies. When the mental battles get tough, reach out for support. Your teammates, friends, or professional allies are your sidekicks in this grand mental quest.

Explore mental health resources available to you. Online therapy, support groups, or even a good old-fashioned chat with a friend (remember that happy hour wine suggestion?) – these resources are the shields and swords in your mental wellness arsenal. Remember, seeking help is not a weakness; it's a demonstration of strength.

Chapter Nine

Networking in a Virtual World

J ust because you're not in the company office daily doesn't mean networking has disappeared. Think of Networking in a virtual world as rubbing virtual elbows with the who's who of your professional realm without leaving the comfort of your home office couch. Our following path in the expedition will be embarking on a networking odyssey.

Overcoming Challenges in Professional Networking: Where Handshakes Are Emoji and Mingling Is Multitasking

Let's face it: virtual networking differs from swanky cocktail parties, where you can effortlessly mingle and exchange business cards. Now, we've got to navigate the digital waters where emojis replace handshakes, and mingling requires serious multitasking skills.

However, you'll soon turn these challenges into opportunities by embracing virtual coffee chats, webinars, and LinkedIn connections. It's networking in your shorts (the longer ones with a belt), and that's a win-win in my book.

Leveraging Virtual Platforms for Networking Success: Your Passport to the Digital Gala

Welcome to the digital gala of networking events! From Zoom to LinkedIn, we've got an array of virtual platforms that can catapult you into the spotlight. Treat these platforms like your networking passports – each with unique perks and quirks.

Optimize your profiles, craft a compelling elevator pitch, and now you can use the line about wearing pants to meetings being a hobby– it's a great ice-breaker! Don't be shy about showcasing your virtual charisma. Change that virtual background from a stack of books to something festive or even a beautiful sunset, and let your skills and personality shine through.

Advancing Your Career in a Remote Setting: Because Climbing the Corporate Ladder Now Involves a Bit of Scrolling

Remote work doesn't mean your career dreams have to take a backseat. In fact, it's an opportunity to redefine how you climb the corporate ladder – one virtual rung at a time.

Attend virtual conferences, participate in online workshops, and engage in industry-specific forums. Classes in public speaking work wonders for your confidence, just as they would in the non-virtual world. Maybe even more so. Become a digital thought leader, sharing your insights and expertise. Before you know it, your LinkedIn notifications will sing with connection requests and career opportunities.

So, my digital mingling marvels, let's make networking in this virtual world our playground. Overcome the challenges, leverage the virtual platforms, and advance your career with strategic scrolling. Networking is no longer about exchanging business cards; it's about leaving a digital footprint that leads straight to your home office door.

Chapter Ten

Crafting a Dedicated Workspace

F or a large percentage of you, welcome to my book! Since you most likely purchased this to figure out how to find the best way to set up and work efficiently in your new home office, you probably came straight to this chapter. I'll try to make it worthwhile and grant the desire to read the rest of it. In this chapter, we don our Fedora (lots of Indiana Jones-ish references throughout; roll with it) to delve into the intricate art of crafting a dedicated workspace. Your home office is not just a place; it's a sanctuary where deadlines meet serenity. So, grab your metaphorical blueprints, and let's build the ultimate fortress of focus and creativity.

Designing and Organizing Your Home Office Space: Where Chaos Meets Creativity

Your home office isn't just a desk and a chair; it's a canvas waiting for your creativity to splash all over it. Designing the perfect workspace is like creating a masterpiece – it requires a touch of chaos and a dash of order. It's also where you'll welcome many clients and coworkers, so it should reflect your persona the same way it would if it were a business office that people walk into daily. As I mentioned, your kitchen is *not* a home office unless you're a chef.

Consider the Feng Shui of your workspace. Position your desk for maximum energy flow. I positioned mine so I could look out the window. Throw in some motivational posters. Mine are airplane cockpit diagrams. And maybe a plant that won't judge you for talking to it. They're great for bouncing ideas off. You would be surprised how often you can solve problems by speaking out loud to a plant. I use a rubber duck; I may be all thumbs occasionally, but none of them is green.

Maximizing Limited Space in Small Living Arrangements: Because Even Harry Potter Managed in a Cupboard

Those tiny home shows are brilliant! I love how they maximize limited space. They turn very small spaces into a cozy haven, and so can you. Recreational vehicles are another excellent example of using small spaces to your advantage.

Invest in multi-functional furniture – a desk that transforms into a dining table or a chair that moonlights as a storage unit. Embrace vertical storage solutions because who says your files can't reach for the stars? Your limited space is a canvas for efficiency and ingenuity.

The Psychological Impact of a Dedicated Workspace: Webcams, microphones, and meetings, oh my!

While your office reflects you, I've only described what you can see. What about what other people see in a meeting? You may recall I mentioned my home office as a "set" in the introduction. I designed my background area so that when on camera, people see items that reflect my professional history, like a visual resume. It provides some icebreakers when meeting with clients and coworkers. Everyone may not have that kind of space, but there is a great alternative.

All the popular meeting software have virtual backgrounds. These provide an excellent opportunity to showcase your personality or set up a meeting theme. I've even gone to the office, taken a photo of the lobby, and used it as my background. The effect is so perfect I've had co-workers ask why I was at the office!

Even with a virtual background, your camera placement is vital! Stop making people look up your nose! Have you ever taken a selfie? Do you shove the camera up your nostril? I didn't think so. Most people open the laptop and think it's all good while the rest of us are counting nose hairs. It's not okay!

You'll want a separate keyboard and monitor, or at least a stand for your laptop that gets the camera to eye level. If your laptop or external monitor has no built-in camera, purchase a good one and put it on the monitor. Take a look at the TV News tonight. Examine how the camera frames the anchor person. You will notice they focus on the person from the shoulders up. They do not put their entire face in the frame, nor should you. Sit back from the camera so people can see from your chest to the top of your head. Your head and eyes should be in the top third of the frame. When placing the camera, line it up directly with your eyes or a little above. It's okay to look slightly up to see the camera; some think it shows off their eyes better. But never, ever look down at your "audience".

Pro Tip: If your web meeting program allows, move the attendees' windows to the top of the screen. Looking at their frame will appear to them as though you are looking directly at them.

Consider an external microphone for the same reason as having a properly placed camera. Just as a proper webcam placement will help, a quality microphone will provide a cleaner sound to your clients and is a very subtle but effective communication tool. There are high-quality ones available for under thirty dollars. When presenting the latest software to a client, you don't want to sound like you're in a tin can.

Taking these steps will increase your client and co-workers' perception of you as a professional. The change is subtle, but we live in an era of movies and TV. We all have a little Hollywood director in us, so let yours shine through.

Chapter Eleven

Putting It All Together

So, my work-from-home trailblazers, we have discussed the remote warrior challenges and discovered some solutions that turn spaces into productivity powerhouses. Whether it's a tiny apartment or a suburban mansion, any space can become the home office of your dreams.

Lessons Learned and Key Takeaways: Wisdom from the Virtual Jungle

We've explored deep into the virtual jungle to find some hidden treasures of wisdom. It's time to fly back home and reflect on all we've covered on our quest for the ultimate home office. From the importance of ergonomic chairs to the magical impact of designated break times, these key takeaways will arm you with the knowledge to conquer your home office challenges.

As we make our final approach, consider how to apply the lessons, embrace the strategies, and add your unique flair to create a home office that reflects your personality and fuels your professional journey.

This plane has landed now, but you are the captain on the next flight. May your journey be filled with peace, productivity, laughter.

You are now free to move about the cabin.

Chapter Twelve

From Explorer to Home Office Warrior

Well, fellow home office adventurers, can you believe we've reached the end of this epic journey? We've covered everything from battling distractions to crafting the ultimate workspace. It's time to wrap up this virtual odyssey with a bang – the conclusion that ties it all together, like the last piece of a jigsaw puzzle.

Reflecting on Your Home Office Evolution: You're Not the Same Remote Warrior You Were Before

Take a moment to reflect on the evolution of your home office. Remember when your desk was a kitchen table, and your coworker was a furry friend? Now, you've gone from an explorer to a seasoned remote warrior, armed with ergonomic chairs, virtual networking skills, and a newfound appreciation for the delicate dance of work and life.

You've faced elephants of distraction, crafted a sanctuary of productivity, and embraced the quirks of virtual networking. You're not just working from home; you're conquering the virtual realm with style, humor, and a touch of strategic genius. Raise a virtual toast to the superhero version of yourself who emerged from the chaos.

Celebrating the Wins, Big and Small: Because Every Completed Task Is a Victory

In the world of remote work, victories come in all shapes and sizes. Whether it's conquering a complex project, turning a household nook into a productivity haven, or mastering the art of virtual networking, every win deserves a celebration.

So, take a victory lap around your home office, throw some metaphorical confetti (or real confetti if you have a robot vacuum), and revel in the fact that you've triumphed over challenges that would make even the members of the Explorer's Club raise an eyebrow. Or not. Anyway, your wins, big and small, are the building blocks of your remote success.

Embracing the Ever-Evolving Nature of Remote Work: Because Change Is the Only Constant

Remember that remote work is a dynamic landscape as we bid farewell to this virtual adventure. Just as the seasons change, so does the nature of our work environments. New challenges will emerge, and fresh opportunities will present themselves.

Embrace the ever-evolving nature of remote work with the resilience of a rubber band – stretch, adapt, and bounce back. Stay curious, stay open to change, and remember that your home office journey is a lifelong adventure with twists, turns, and the occasional surprise cameo from your pet during an important video call.

The Future Is Yours to Craft: Write the Next Chapter of Your Remote Odyssey

And now, my virtual companions, it's time for you to wield your metaphorical pens and write the next chapter of your remote odyssey. Armed with the lessons, strategies, and humor from our shared adventure, the future of your home office is in your hands.

Craft a workspace that fuels your professional aspirations and nourishes your well-being. Infuse your remote journey with the spirit of creativity, the power of resilience, and a generous sprinkle of humor. Your home office is not just a space; it's a canvas for your continued growth and success.

So, my friends, may your Wi-Fi be strong, your morning beverage be hot, and your productivity soar to new heights. The virtual realm is yours to conquer. And, if you found this book helpful, please be my personal superhero and leave a favorable review on Amazon.

Chapter Thirteen

References

Writing this book involved creativity, general knowledge, and everyday advice from various resources. However, since the content combines original material and general knowledge, there are no specific resources to cite. The information provided results from synthesizing multiple concepts, ideas, and knowledge.

For further information on topics of setting up a home office, ergonomic practices, mental wellness, and remote work strategies, you will find valuable insights from reputable sources such as:

1. Occupational Safety and Health Administration (OSHA) guidelines for ergonomic practices.

2. Articles and tips from productivity and remote work experts on platforms like Harvard Business Review, Forbes, and Fast Company.

3. Insights on mental health and well-being from reputable sources like the World Health Organization (WHO) or mental health organizations.

4. Home office setup advice from furniture manufacturers, ergonomic product providers, and workspace design experts.

5. Business and career development advice from reputable LinkedIn Learning, Udemy, or Coursera platforms.